OVERNIC

OATS

RECIPE

Quick and Easy, Traditional to Modern, Energizing, and Mouthwatering recipes

by

Refferd Edwin

Copyright

Copyright © 2024 by Refferd Edwin

Table of Contents

Introduction to Overnight Oats

Welcome to the fantastic world of overnight oats! We will explore this adored morning meal choice's history, advantages, and appeal. Overnight oats have become popular in recent years, and for good cause. They provide a simple, healthy, and tasty way to start your day on the right foot.

Origins and Evolution:

Soaking oats overnight has existed for generations, with origins reaching back to traditional Swiss muesli. However, the modern adaptation of overnight oats has converted this essential meal into a mainstay of contemporary morning culture. From its modest origins to its prominence as a morning superstar, overnight oats have experienced a remarkable metamorphosis.

The Appeal of Overnight Oats:

What makes overnight oats so unique? One of its most tempting aspects is its convenience. With minimum prep work necessary the night before, you may wake up to a tasty breakfast from the fridge. Additionally, overnight oats are incredibly adaptable, enabling you to adjust them to your taste preferences and dietary requirements. Whether vegan, gluten-free, or just desiring an excellent breakfast, overnight oats have you covered.

The Health Factor:

Beyond their convenience and adaptability, overnight oats are filled with nutritious advantages. They're a good source of fiber, which supports digestive health and helps keep you full and pleased until your next meal. Additionally, overnight oats may be fortified with a range of healthy add-ins, such as fruits, nuts, seeds, and protein powders, to improve their nutritional value further.

Join the Overnight Oats Revolution:

As you begin your overnight oats adventure, expect to be inspired by the many possibilities that await you. Whether you're a seasoned oatmeal lover or new to overnight oats, transform your morning routine with this simple but spectacular dish.

Benefits of Overnight Oats

we'll investigate the myriad advantages that overnight oats have to offer. From their convenience to their nutritious benefits, overnight oats have earned their proper position as a breakfast favorite for numerous folks worldwide.

Convenience at Its Best:
One of the most significant benefits of overnight oats is their convenience. By preparing your breakfast the night before, you may save considerable time in the morning, enabling you to enjoy a leisurely meal without a hurry. Whether you're a busy professional, a mom on the road, or someone who wants additional sleep, overnight oats are a godsend.

Nutritional Powerhouse:
In addition to being handy, overnight oats are also highly healthy. They're a good source of fiber, which improves digestive health and helps manage blood sugar levels. Furthermore, overnight oats may be modified with a range of healthy add-ins, such as fruits, nuts, seeds, and superfoods, to improve their nutritional value further.

Versatility and Customization:
Another advantage of overnight oats is their adaptability. With various flavor combinations, you can tailor your oats to fit your taste preferences and nutritional demands. Whether you favor sweet or savory, fruity or nutty, there's an overnight oats recipe for everyone.

Sustainable and Budget-Friendly:
Finally, overnight oats are a sustainable and budget-friendly breakfast alternative. Oats are an economic pantry staple that can be bought in bulk, making them a cost-effective solution for budget-conscious folks. Additionally, making breakfast at home may limit food waste and lessen your environmental imprint.

Getting Started: Basic Overnight Oats Recipe

Embarking on your overnight oats adventure can be simple. In truth, it's as easy as mixing a few crucial elements and letting time work its magic. This chapter will lead you through the simplest method of cooking overnight oats, outlining crucial processes and presenting you with a basic recipe to begin your mornings.

How to Start:
Starting your overnight oats journey is as simple as grabbing a few core ingredients and a jar with a cover. Choose a mason jar, a reusable container, or any receptacle that can be shut firmly to keep your oats fresh while they soak.

Easy Way to Start:
If you're new to overnight oats, don't worry! The technique is essential and involves minimum effort. Mix oats, liquid, and any desired add-ins in your selected container, give it a good stir, chill overnight, and wake up to a lovely breakfast waiting for you.

Essential Things to Do:
While preparing overnight oats is straightforward, there are a few crucial factors to consider for maximum results. First, pick the correct variety of oats—rolled or old-fashioned oats work best since they soften nicely when soaked overnight. Secondly, check you have the proper ratio of oats to liquid to obtain the required consistency. Finally, don't forget to chill your oats for at least 4-6 hours to enable them to soften and absorb the flavors.

Basic Overnight Oats Recipe

Ingredients:
♡ 1/2 cup rolled oats
♡ 1/2 cup milk (dairy or plant-based)
♡ 1/4 cup Greek yogurt (optional for added creaminess)
♡ One tablespoon of honey or maple syrup (optional for sweetness)
♡ Pinch of salt

Optional add-ins:
♡ Sliced fruits, nuts, seeds, spices, or flavorings of your choice.

Instructions:
⚡ In a mason jar or container with a lid, mix the rolled oats, milk, Greek yogurt (if using), honey or maple syrup (if using), and a sprinkle of salt. Stir carefully to ensure all components are well blended.

⚡ Add any desired add-ins to the oats mixture, such as sliced fruits, nuts, seeds, spices, or flavorings. Stir until all ingredients are uniformly distributed throughout the oats mixture.

Seal the jar or container with a lid and refrigerate overnight, or for at least 4-6 hours, to enable the oats to soften and absorb the flavors.

⚡ In the morning, toss the oats thoroughly to combine any separated ingredients. If desired, add extra toppings or sweeteners to taste.

⚡ Enjoy your delicious and healthy basic overnight oats directly from the fridge, or let them get to room temperature if desired.

With this basic recipe as your base, you can alter your overnight oats to fit your taste preferences and nutritional demands. Get creative with your add-ins and toppings and start your mornings with a beautiful and healthful breakfast ready when you are.

Rolled Oats Recipes

Classic Overnight Oats

Ingredients:
- ♡ 1/2 cup rolled oats
- ♡ 1/2 cup milk (dairy or plant-based)
- ♡ 1/4 cup Greek yogurt (optional)
- ♡ One tablespoon of honey or maple syrup (optional)
- ♡ Pinch of salt

Directions:
- ⚡ Add oats, milk, Greek yogurt (if using), honey or maple syrup (if using), and salt to a dish or mason jar.
- ⚡ Stir well to mix.
- ⚡ Cover and refrigerate overnight or for at least 4-6 hours.
- ⚡ In the morning, toss the oats and add toppings as desired.

Benefits:
Classic overnight oats provide a creamy, comforting breakfast choice that can be easily modified with your favorite toppings. They deliver lasting energy and critical nutrients for a productive day ahead.

Blueberry Almond Overnight Oats

Ingredients:
- ♡ 1/2 cup rolled oats
- ♡ 1/2 cup almond milk
- ♡ 1/4 cup Greek yogurt
- ♡ One tablespoon of almond butter
- ♡ One tablespoon honey
- ♡ 1/4 teaspoon almond extract (optional)
- ♡ 1/4 cup fresh or frozen blueberries
- ♡ Sliced almonds for garnish

Directions:

⚡ Add oats, almond milk, Greek yogurt, almond butter, honey, and almond extract (if using) in a dish or mason jar.

⚡ Stir well to mix.

⚡ Gently fold in blueberries.

⚡ Cover and refrigerate overnight.

⚡ In the morning, mix the oats and sprinkle with sliced almonds before eating.

Benefits:

Blueberry almond overnight oats combine a delectable combination of nutty tastes and bursts of sweetness from blueberries. They also provide a high supply of fiber, antioxidants, and healthy fats to promote general health and well-being.

Peanut Butter Banana Overnight Oats

Ingredients:

♡ 1/2 cup rolled oats
♡ 1/2 cup milk (dairy or plant-based)
♡ 1/4 cup Greek yogurt
♡ One tablespoon of peanut butter
♡ One tablespoon of honey or maple syrup
♡ 1/2 ripe banana, mashed
♡ Sliced banana, for garnish (optional)
♡ Drizzle additional peanut butter for garnish (optional)

Directions:

⚡ Add oats, milk, Greek yogurt, peanut butter, honey or maple syrup, and mashed banana to a blow or mason jar.

⚡ Stir well to mix.

⚡ Cover and refrigerate overnight.

⚡ Mix the oats and top with sliced banana and peanut butter drizzle in the morning.

Chocolate Coconut Overnight Oats

Ingredients:
- ♡ 1/2 cup rolled oats
- ♡ 1/2 cup coconut milk
- ♡ 1/4 cup Greek yogurt
- ♡ One tablespoon of cocoa powder
- ♡ One tablespoon of honey or maple syrup
- ♡ Two tablespoons shredded coconut
- ♡ Dark chocolate shavings for garnish (optional)

Directions:
⚡ Add oats, coconut milk, Greek yogurt, cocoa powder, honey or maple syrup, or shredded coconut to a dish or mason jar.
⚡ Stir well to mix.
⚡ Cover and refrigerate overnight.
⚡ Mix the oats and top with dark chocolate shavings in the morning, if preferred.

Benefits:
Chocolate coconut overnight oats provide a luxurious and indulgent taste combination. They deliver a rich supply of antioxidants from cocoa powder and healthy fats from coconut milk while boosting satiety and pleasure througho the morning.

Raspberry Vanilla Overnight Oats

Ingredients:
- ♡ 1/2 cup rolled oats
- ♡ 1/2 cup milk (dairy or plant-based)
- ♡ 1/4 cup Greek yogurt
- ♡ One tablespoon of honey or maple syrup
- ♡ 1/2 teaspoon vanilla extract
- ♡ 1/4 cup fresh or frozen raspberries
- ♡ Fresh raspberries, for garnish (optional)

Directions:
- ⚡ Combine oats, milk, Greek yogurt, honey or maple syrup, and vanilla extract in a bowl or mason jar.
- ⚡ Stir well to combine.
- ⚡ Gently fold in raspberries.
- ⚡ Cover and refrigerate overnight.
- ⚡ In the morning, stir the oats and top with fresh raspberries, if desired.

Benefits:
Overnight oats with raspberry vanilla provide a perfect combination of acidity from the raspberries and sweetness from the honey and vanilla, creating a refreshing and fulfilling breakfast alternative filled with fiber, vitamins, and antioxidants.

Apple Cinnamon Overnight Oats

Ingredients:
- ♡ 1/2 cup rolled oats
- ♡ 1/2 cup milk (dairy or plant-based)
- ♡ 1/4 cup unsweetened applesauce
- ♡ 1/4 cup Greek yogurt
- ♡ One tablespoon of honey or maple syrup
- ♡ 1/2 teaspoon ground cinnamon
- ♡ 1/4 cup diced apple
- ♡ Chopped walnuts for garnish (optional)

Directions:

⚡ Add oats, milk, applesauce, Greek yogurt, honey or maple syrup, and ground cinnamon to a dish or mason jar.

⚡ Stir well to mix.

⚡ Gently fold in a diced apple.

⚡ Cover and refrigerate overnight.

⚡ Mix the oats and top with chopped walnuts in the morning, if preferred.

Benefits:

Apple cinnamon overnight oats provide a pleasant combination of toasty spices and delicious apples. They also provide a rich dose of fiber, vitamins, and minerals to help digestion and immunological health.

Mango Pineapple Overnight Oats

Ingredients:

♡ 1/2 cup rolled oats

♡ 1/2 cup coconut milk

♡ 1/4 cup Greek yogurt

♡ 1/4 cup diced mango

♡ 1/4 cup diced pineapple

♡ One tablespoon of honey or maple syrup

♡ Toasted coconut flakes for garnish (optional)

Directions:

⚡ Add oats, coconut milk, Greek yogurt, chopped mango, diced pineapple, and honey or maple syrup to a dish or mason jar.

⚡ Stir well to mix.

⚡ Cover and refrigerate overnight.

⚡ Mix the oats and top with toasted coconut flakes in the morning, if preferred.

Benefits:
Mango pineapple overnight oats give a tropical vacation with sweet and tangy tastes, delivering a refreshing and nutrient-rich breakfast alternative filled with vitamin C, fiber, and antioxidants for maximum health and vitality.

Pecan Pie Overnight Oats

Ingredients:
- ♡ 1/2 cup rolled oats
- ♡ 1/2 cup milk (dairy or plant-based)
- ♡ 1/4 cup Greek yogurt
- ♡ One tablespoon of maple syrup
- ♡ 1/4 teaspoon vanilla extract
- ♡ Two tablespoons chopped pecans
- ♡ Dash of cinnamon
- ♡ Maple syrup for drizzling (optional)

Directions:
- ⚡ Add oats, milk, Greek yogurt, maple syrup, vanilla essence, chopped nuts, and cinnamon in a dish or mason jar.
- ⚡ Stir well to mix.
- ⚡ Cover and refrigerate overnight.
- ⚡ Mix the oats and sprinkle with maple syrup in the morning, if preferred.

Benefits:
Pecan pie overnight oats give the soothing aromas of a traditional dessert, delivering a rich amount of healthy fats, protein, and fiber from pecans, coupled with a touch of sweetness from maple syrup, for a fulfilling and decadent morning delight.

Lemon Poppy Seed Overnight Oats

Ingredients:
- ♡ 1/2 cup rolled oats
- ♡ 1/2 cup milk (dairy or plant-based)
- ♡ 1/4 cup Greek yogurt
- ♡ One tablespoon of honey or maple syrup
- ♡ Zest of 1 lemon
- ♡ One tablespoon of fresh lemon juice
- ♡ 1/2 teaspoon poppy seeds
- ♡ Sliced lemon, for garnish (optional)

Directions:
⚡ Add oats, milk, Greek yogurt, honey or maple syrup, lemon zest, lemon juice, and poppy seeds in a dish or mason jar.
⚡ Stir well to mix.
⚡ Cover and refrigerate overnight.
⚡ Mix the oats and garnish with sliced lemon in the morning, if preferred.

Benefits:
Lemon poppy seed overnight oats deliver a crisp blast of citrus flavor and a lovely crunch from the poppy seeds. They also offer a dose of vitamin C, antioxidants, and fiber for a refreshing and energetic start to the day.

Maple Walnut Overnight Oats

Ingredients:
- ♡ 1/2 cup rolled oats
- ♡ 1/2 cup milk (dairy or plant-based)
- ♡ 1/4 cup Greek yogurt
- ♡ One tablespoon of maple syrup
- ♡ 1/4 teaspoon vanilla extract
- ♡ Two tablespoons chopped walnuts
- ♡ Pinch of cinnamon

18

♡ Extra maple syrup for drizzling (optional)

Directions:
⚡ Add oats, milk, Greek yogurt, maple syrup, vanilla essence, chopped walnuts, and a sprinkle of cinnamon to a plate or mason jar.
⚡ Stir thoroughly to combine.
⚡ Cover and refrigerate overnight.
⚡ In the morning, stir the oats and sprinkle with more maple syrup, if desired.

Benefits:
Maple walnut overnight oats are a great blend of sweet maple flavor and crunchy walnuts. They deliver many omega-3 fatty acids, antioxidants, and fiber for heart health and brain function, making them a pleasant and full morning option.

Old-Fashioned Oats Recipes

Mixed Berry Overnight Oats

Ingredients:
- ♡ 1/2 cup rolled oats
- ♡ 1/2 cup milk (dairy or plant-based)
- ♡ 1/4 cup Greek yogurt
- ♡ One tablespoon of honey or maple syrup
- ♡ 1/2 cup mixed berries (such as strawberries, blueberries, raspberries)
- ♡ Fresh mint leaves, for garnish (optional)

Directions:
- ⚡ Mix oats, milk, Greek yogurt, and honey or maple syrup a dish or mason jar.
- ⚡ Stir well to mix.
- ⚡ Gently fold in mixed berries.
- ⚡ Cover and refrigerate overnight.
- ⚡ In the morning, mix the oats and sprinkle with fresh min leaves, if preferred.

Benefits:
Mixed berry overnight oats provide a refreshing and natura sweet taste profile, rich with antioxidants, vitamins, and fib to enhance general health and well-being.

Pumpkin Spice Overnight Oats

Ingredients:
- ♡ 1/2 cup rolled oats
- ♡ 1/2 cup milk (dairy or plant-based)
- ♡ 1/4 cup pumpkin puree
- ♡ 1/4 cup Greek yogurt
- ♡ One tablespoon of maple syrup or honey
- ♡ 1/2 teaspoon pumpkin pie spice
- ♡ Pumpkin seeds, for garnish (optional)

Directions:

⚡ Add oats, milk, pumpkin puree, Greek yogurt, maple syrup or honey, and pumpkin pie spice in a bowl or mason jar.

⚡ Stir well to mix.

⚡ Cover and refrigerate overnight.

⚡ Mix the oats and top with pumpkin seeds in the morning, if preferred.

Benefits:

Pumpkin spice overnight oats give a pleasant and soothing taste evocative of autumn while delivering a healthy dose of fiber, vitamins, and minerals to promote immune health and digestion.

Cherry Almond Overnight Oats

Ingredients:

♡ 1/2 cup rolled oats

♡ 1/2 cup almond milk

♡ 1/4 cup Greek yogurt

♡ One tablespoon of honey or maple syrup

♡ 1/4 teaspoon almond extract

♡ 1/4 cup cherries, pitted and halved

♡ Sliced almonds for garnish (optional)

Directions:

⚡ Almond milk, Greek yogurt, honey or maple syrup, almond extract, and oats should all be combined in a mason jar or dish.

⚡ Mix well to blend.

⚡ Stir in cherries gently.

⚡ Refrigerate overnight with a cover on.

⚡ Stir the oats and sprinkle some almond slices on top if you'd like in the morning.

Benefits:
In addition to being an excellent source of antioxidants, heart-healthy fats, and protein to promote muscle repair and heart health, cherry almond overnight oats have a delicious blend of nutty and fruity tastes.

Banana Bread Overnight Oats

Ingredients:
- ♡ 1/2 cup rolled oats
- ♡ 1/2 cup milk (dairy or plant-based)
- ♡ 1/4 cup Greek yogurt
- ♡ 1/2 ripe banana, mashed
- ♡ One tablespoon of honey or maple syrup
- ♡ 1/4 teaspoon ground cinnamon
- ♡ Chopped walnuts for garnish (optional)
- ♡ Sliced banana, for garnish (optional)

Directions:
⚡ Oats, milk, Greek yogurt, mashed banana, honey, maple syrup, and ground cinnamon should all be combined in a bowl or mason jar.

⚡ Mix well to blend.

⚡ Refrigerate overnight with a cover on.

⚡ Stir the oats in the morning, and if you'd like, top with sliced banana and chopped walnuts.

Benefits:
Banana bread overnight oats are a healthy breakfast alternative that smells like homemade banana bread. They are high in potassium, fiber, and carbohydrates, which give you energy to get through the day.

Coconut Lime Overnight Oats

Ingredients:
♡ 1/2 cup rolled oats
♡ 1/2 cup coconut milk
♡ 1/4 cup Greek yogurt
♡ One tablespoon of honey or maple syrup
♡ Zest and juice of 1 lime
♡ Two tablespoons shredded coconut
♡ Sliced lime, for garnish (optional)

Directions:
⚡ Combine oats, Greek yogurt, coconut milk, honey, maple syrup, zest, lime juice, and shredded coconut in a bowl or mason jar.
⚡ Mix well to blend.
⚡ Refrigerate overnight with a cover on.
⚡ Stir the oats and add some sliced lime, if you'd like, in the morning.

Benefits:
In addition to offering a tasty and tropical taste combination, coconut lime overnight oats are a fantastic source of healthy fats, vitamin C, and electrolytes to promote skin health and hydration.

Carrot Cake Overnight Oats

Ingredients:
♡ 1/2 cup rolled oats
♡ 1/2 cup milk (dairy or plant-based)
♡ 1/4 cup Greek yogurt
♡ One tablespoon of honey or maple syrup
♡ 1/4 cup shredded carrot
♡ 1/4 teaspoon ground cinnamon
♡ Chopped walnuts or pecans for garnish (optional)
♡ Raisins, for garnish (optional)

Directions:

⚡ Combine oats, milk, Greek yogurt, honey, maple syrup, shredded carrot, and ground cinnamon in a bowl or mason jar.

⚡ Mix well to blend.

⚡ Refrigerate overnight with a cover on.

⚡ Stir the oats in the morning, and if you like, top with chopped pecans, walnuts, or raisins.

Benefits:

Carrot cake overnight oats are a healthy breakfast alternative that offers all the delicious tastes of a traditional dessert, with the added benefits of beta-carotene, fiber, and antioxidants for maximum health and energy.

Cranberry Orange Overnight Oats

Ingredients:

♡ 1/2 cup rolled oats

♡ 1/2 cup milk (dairy or plant-based)

♡ 1/4 cup Greek yogurt

♡ One tablespoon of honey or maple syrup

♡ Zest and juice of 1 orange

♡ Two tablespoons dried cranberries

♡ Sliced almonds for garnish (optional)

♡ Fresh orange segments for garnish (optional)

Directions:

⚡ Combine oats, milk, Greek yogurt, honey, maple syrup, orange zest, juice, and dried cranberries in a bowl or mason jar.

⚡ Mix well to blend.

⚡ Refrigerate overnight with a cover on.

⚡ Stir the oats in the morning, and if you'd like, top with sliced almonds and fresh orange segments.

Benefits:

In addition to offering a delicious citrus taste and acidity from the cranberries, cranberry orange overnight oats are a fantastic source of vitamin C, antioxidants, and immune-boosting qualities to promote general health and well-being.

Chocolate Cherry Overnight Oats

Ingredients:

- ♡ 1/2 cup rolled oats
- ♡ 1/2 cup milk (dairy or plant-based)
- ♡ 1/4 cup Greek yogurt
- ♡ One tablespoon of honey or maple syrup
- ♡ One tablespoon of cocoa powder
- ♡ 1/4 teaspoon vanilla extract
- ♡ 1/4 cup chopped cherries
- ♡ Dark chocolate shavings for garnish (optional)

Directions:

⚡ Combine oats, milk, Greek yogurt, honey (or maple syrup), chocolate powder, and vanilla extract in a bowl or mason jar.

⚡ Mix well to blend.

⚡ Stir in chopped cherries gently.

⚡ Refrigerate overnight with a cover on.

⚡ Stir the oats and sprinkle some dark chocolate shavings on top if you'd like in the morning.

Benefits:

In addition to being rich in antioxidants, fiber, and vital minerals that promote heart health and satisfy chocolate cravings, chocolate cherry overnight oats are a satisfying and luxurious breakfast alternative.

Peach Cobbler Overnight Oats

Ingredients:
♡ 1/2 cup rolled oats
♡ 1/2 cup milk (dairy or plant-based)
♡ 1/4 cup Greek yogurt
♡ One tablespoon of honey or maple syrup
♡ 1/4 teaspoon ground cinnamon
♡ 1/2 cup diced peaches (fresh or frozen)
♡ Granola, for garnish (optional)

Directions:
⚡ Combine oats, milk, Greek yogurt, honey, maple syrup, and ground cinnamon in a bowl or mason jar.
⚡ Mix well to blend.
⚡ Fold in sliced peaches gently.
⚡ Refrigerate overnight with a cover on.
⚡ Stir the oats and add granola if you'd like in the morning

Benefits:
Peach cobbler overnight oats evoke a traditional dessert's sweet and cozy aromas. They also contain antioxidants, fiber, and vitamin C to aid digestion and increase fullness throughout the morning.

Blueberry Lemon Overnight Oats

Ingredients:
♡ 1/2 cup rolled oats
♡ 1/2 cup milk (dairy or plant-based)
♡ 1/4 cup Greek yogurt
♡ One tablespoon of honey or maple syrup
♡ Zest and juice of 1/2 lemon
♡ 1/4 cup fresh or frozen blueberries
♡ Lemon slices, for garnish (optional)

Directions:

⚡ Add oats, milk, Greek yogurt, honey, maple syrup, lemon zest, and lemon juice in a bowl or mason jar.

⚡ To blend, thoroughly mix.

⚡ Gently fold in blueberries.

⚡ Cover and refrigerate overnight.

⚡ In the morning, stir the oats and, if desired, add some lemon slices.

Benefits:

Blueberry lemon overnight oats provide a delightful and zesty flavor combination. They are also an excellent source of vitamin C, antioxidants, and fiber, which promote immune health and encourage a bright and refreshing start to your day.

Sweet Overnight Oats Recipes

Chocolate Peanut Butter Cup Overnight Oats

Ingredients:
♡ 1/2 cup rolled oats
♡ 1/2 cup milk (dairy or plant-based)
♡ 1/4 cup Greek yogurt
♡ One tablespoon of cocoa powder
♡ One tablespoon of peanut butter
♡ One tablespoon of honey or maple syrup
♡ Mini chocolate chips for garnish (optional)

Directions:
⚡ Mix the oats, milk, Greek yogurt, cocoa powder, peanut butter, honey, or maple syrup in a dish or mason jar.
⚡ To blend, thoroughly mix.
⚡ Cover and refrigerate overnight.
⚡ Mix the oats and garnish with a little chocolate chip in the morning, if desired.

Benefits:
A great source of protein, fiber, and antioxidants, chocolate peanut butter cup overnight oats provide a luxurious and indulgent taste combination that satisfies cravings and encourages satiety throughout the morning.

Blueberry Lemon Overnight Oats

Ingredients:
♡ 1/2 cup rolled oats
♡ 1/2 cup milk (dairy or plant-based)
♡ 1/4 cup Greek yogurt
♡ One tablespoon of honey or maple syrup
♡ Zest and juice of 1/2 lemon
♡ 1/4 cup fresh or frozen blueberries

♡ Lemon slices, for garnish (optional)

Directions:
⚡ Oats, milk, Greek yogurt, honey, maple syrup, lemon zest, and lemon juice should all be combined in a bowl or mason jar.
⚡ Mix well to blend.
⚡ Fold in blueberries gently.
⚡ Refrigerate overnight with a cover on.
⚡ Stir the oats in the morning and add some lemon slices if you'd like.

Benefits:
Blueberry lemon overnight oats are a great source of vitamin C, antioxidants, and fiber, which support immune health and encourage a bright and energizing start to your day. They also provide a pleasant and tangy taste combination.

Banana Nutella Overnight Oats

Ingredients:

♡ 1/2 cup rolled oats
♡ 1/2 cup milk (dairy or plant-based)
♡ 1/4 cup Greek yogurt
♡ 1/2 ripe banana, mashed
♡ One tablespoon Nutella (or hazelnut spread)
♡ One tablespoon of honey or maple syrup
♡ Sliced banana and chopped hazelnuts for garnish (optional)

Directions:
⚡ Oats, milk, Greek yogurt, mashed banana, Nutella, and honey or maple syrup should all be combined in a bowl or mason jar.
⚡ Mix well to blend.
⚡ Refrigerate overnight with a cover on.
⚡ Stir the oats in the morning and top with chopped hazelnuts and sliced banana.

Benefits:

For a filling and tasty breakfast, banana Nutella overnight oats combine creamy banana and decadent chocolate hazelnut flavors. They are also an excellent source of potassium, antioxidants, and carbs that promote energy.

Apple Cinnamon Overnight Oats

Ingredients:

- ♡ 1/2 cup rolled oats
- ♡ 1/2 cup milk (dairy or plant-based)
- ♡ 1/4 cup unsweetened applesauce
- ♡ 1/4 cup Greek yogurt
- ♡ One tablespoon of honey or maple syrup
- ♡ 1/2 teaspoon ground cinnamon
- ♡ 1/4 cup diced apple
- ♡ Chopped walnuts for garnish (optional)

Directions:

⚡ Oats, milk, applesauce, Greek yogurt, honey, maple syrup, and ground cinnamon should all be combined in a bowl or mason jar.

⚡ Mix well to blend.

⚡ Fold in the diced apple gently.

⚡ Refrigerate overnight with a cover on.

⚡ Stir the oats and sprinkle chopped walnuts on top if you'd like in the morning.

Benefits:

Apple cinnamon overnight oats offer a comforting and classic flavor combination. They are also a good source of fiber, vitamins, and antioxidants to support digestion and promote satiety throughout the morning.

Strawberry Cheesecake Overnight Oats

Ingredients:

♡ 1/2 cup rolled oats
♡ 1/2 cup milk (dairy or plant-based)
♡ 1/4 cup Greek yogurt
♡ One tablespoon of honey or maple syrup
♡ 1/4 teaspoon vanilla extract
♡ 1/4 cup diced strawberries
♡ Graham cracker crumbs for garnish (optional)

Directions:

⚡ Combine oats, milk, Greek yogurt, honey, maple syrup, and vanilla extract in a bowl or mason jar.
⚡ Mix well to blend.
⚡ Stir in chopped strawberries gently.
⚡ Refrigerate overnight with a cover on.
⚡ Stir the oats and sprinkle graham cracker crumbs on top if you'd like in the morning.

Benefits:

A lovely combination of creamy texture and sweet berry taste, strawberry cheesecake overnight oats are a fantastic source of protein, calcium, and antioxidants, making them a filling and healthy breakfast option that will make you nostalgic for your favorite dessert.

Almond Joy Overnight Oats

Ingredients:

♡ 1/2 cup rolled oats
♡ 1/2 cup coconut milk
♡ 1/4 cup Greek yogurt
♡ One tablespoon of cocoa powder
♡ One tablespoon of honey or maple syrup
♡ Two tablespoons shredded coconut
♡ Two tablespoons chopped almonds
♡ Dark chocolate shavings for garnish (optional)

Directions:

⚡ Oats, coconut milk, Greek yogurt, cocoa powder, honey or maple syrup, shredded coconut, and sliced almonds should all be combined in a bowl or mason jar.

⚡ Mix well to blend.

⚡ Refrigerate overnight with a cover on.

⚡ Stir the oats and sprinkle some dark chocolate shavings on top if you'd like in the morning.

Benefits:

In addition to offering a rich and gratifying chocolate, coconut, and almond taste combination, Almond Joy overnight oats are a fantastic source of fiber, antioxidants, and healthy fats that promote general health and well-being

Peach Cobbler Overnight Oats

Ingredients:

♡ 1/2 cup rolled oats

♡ 1/2 cup milk (dairy or plant-based)

♡ 1/4 cup Greek yogurt

♡ One tablespoon of honey or maple syrup

♡ 1/4 teaspoon ground cinnamon

♡ 1/2 cup diced peaches (fresh or frozen)

♡ Granola, for garnish (optional)

Directions:

⚡ Combine oats, milk, Greek yogurt, honey, maple syrup, and ground cinnamon in a bowl or mason jar.

⚡ Mix well to blend.

⚡ Fold in sliced peaches gently.

⚡ Refrigerate overnight with a cover on.

⚡ Stir the oats and add granola if you'd like in the morning

Benefits:

Peach cobbler overnight oats evoke a traditional dessert's sweet and cozy aromas. They also contain antioxidants, fiber, and vitamin C to aid digestion and increase fullness throughout the morning.

Raspberry Dark Chocolate Overnight Oats

Ingredients:

- ♡ 1/2 cup rolled oats
- ♡ 1/2 cup milk (dairy or plant-based)
- ♡ 1/4 cup Greek yogurt
- ♡ One tablespoon of honey or maple syrup
- ♡ One tablespoon of cocoa powder
- ♡ 1/4 cup fresh raspberries
- ♡ Dark chocolate chips or chunks for garnish (optional)

Directions:

⚡ Oats, milk, Greek yogurt, honey, maple syrup, and cocoa powder should all be combined in a bowl or mason jar.

⚡ Mix well to blend.

⚡ Fold in the fresh raspberries gently.

⚡ Refrigerate overnight with a cover on.

⚡ Stir the oats in the morning and add some dark chocolate chunks or chips on top if you'd like.

Benefits:

In addition to offering a rich and decadent taste combination, raspberry dark chocolate overnight oats are an excellent source of fiber, antioxidants, and other vital nutrients that can satisfy cravings and promote general health and well-being.

Coconut Mango Overnight Oats

Ingredients:
- ♡ 1/2 cup rolled oats
- ♡ 1/2 cup coconut milk
- ♡ 1/4 cup Greek yogurt
- ♡ One tablespoon of honey or maple syrup
- ♡ 1/4 cup diced mango
- ♡ Two tablespoons shredded coconut
- ♡ Sliced mango for garnish (optional)

Directions:
⚡ Combine oats, Greek yogurt, coconut milk, honey, maple syrup, sliced mango, and shredded coconut in a mason jar or dish.
⚡ Mix well to blend.
⚡ Refrigerate overnight with a cover on.
⚡ Stir the oats in the morning and add some mango slices if you'd like.

Benefits:
With a creamy coconut base and sweet mango chunks, coconut mango overnight oats provide a taste of the tropics. They're also a fantastic source of vitamin C, fiber, and healthy fats to promote immune system function and sustain energy levels throughout the day.

Maple Pecan Overnight Oats

Ingredients:
- ♡ 1/2 cup rolled oats
- ♡ 1/2 cup milk (dairy or plant-based)
- ♡ 1/4 cup Greek yogurt
- ♡ One tablespoon of maple syrup
- ♡ 1/4 teaspoon vanilla extract
- ♡ Two tablespoons chopped pecans
- ♡ Maple syrup for drizzling (optional)

Directions:

⚡ Mix the oats, milk, Greek yogurt, maple syrup, vanilla extract, and a jar or bowl.

⚡ Mix well to blend.

⚡ Stir in chopped pecans gently.

⚡ Refrigerate overnight with a cover on.

⚡ Stir the oats and, if desired, sprinkle with more maple syrup in the morning.

Benefits:

In addition to providing a rich amount of protein, fiber, and other nutrients to promote general health and well-being, maple pecan overnight oats fulfill your sweet tooth with natural sweetness from maple syrup. They also give a comfortable and nutritious taste combination.

Savory Overnight Oats Recipes

Mediterranean Savory Oats with Feta and Olives

Ingredients:
- ♡ 1/2 cup rolled oats
- ♡ 1/2 cup vegetable broth
- ♡ 1/4 cup Greek yogurt
- ♡ Two tablespoons of crumbled feta cheese
- ♡ One tablespoon chopped Kalamata olives
- ♡ One tablespoon of chopped sun-dried tomatoes
- ♡ One tablespoon of chopped fresh parsley
- ♡ Salt and pepper to taste

Directions:
⚡ Place the veggie broth and rolled oats in a jar or dish.
⚡ Add the sun-dried tomatoes, chopped olives, Greek yogurt, crumbled feta cheese, fresh parsley and stir.
⚡ To taste, add salt and pepper for seasoning.
⚡ Refrigerate overnight with a cover on.
⚡ Stir the oats and adjust the seasoning if necessary in the morning.
⚡ As desired, serve warm or cold.

Benefits:
Mediterranean savory oats are a great source of protein, healthy fats, and fiber to keep you full and energetic throughout the morning. They have a savory and tangy taste profile with a blast of Mediterranean-inspired ingredients.

Mexican-inspired Black Bean and Corn Overnight Oats

Ingredients:
- ♡ 1/2 cup rolled oats
- ♡ 1/2 cup vegetable broth
- ♡ 1/4 cup Greek yogurt
- ♡ Two tablespoons of black beans rinsed and drained
- ♡ Two tablespoons of corn kernels (fresh or canned)
- ♡ One tablespoon chopped fresh cilantro
- ♡ One tablespoon salsa
- ♡ 1/4 teaspoon ground cumin
- ♡ Salt and pepper to taste

Directions:
- ⚡ Place the veggie broth and rolled oats in a jar or dish.
- ⚡ Add the salsa, ground cumin, chopped cilantro, Greek yogurt, black beans, corn kernels, and salt and pepper.
- ⚡ Refrigerate overnight with a cover on.
- ⚡ Stir the oats and adjust the seasoning if necessary in the morning.
- ⚡ As desired, serve warm or cold.

Benefits:
Black bean and corn overnight oats with a Mexican flair have a savory, spicy taste profile with a sweetness from the corn. They are a great source of fiber, protein, and other vital elements to help maintain a balanced, healthful diet.

Savory Parmesan and Herb Overnight Oats

Ingredients:
- ♡ 1/2 cup rolled oats
- ♡ 1/2 cup vegetable broth
- ♡ 1/4 cup Greek yogurt
- ♡ Two tablespoons of grated Parmesan cheese
- ♡ One tablespoon chopped fresh herbs (parsley, basil, or chives)
- ♡ 1/4 teaspoon garlic powder

♡ Salt and pepper to taste

Directions:

⚡ Place the veggie broth and rolled oats in a jar or dish.
⚡ Add the chopped fresh herbs, Greek yogurt, grated Parmesan cheese, garlic powder, salt, and pepper and stir.
⚡ Refrigerate overnight with a cover on.
⚡ Stir the oats and adjust the seasoning if necessary in the morning.
⚡ As desired, serve warm or cold.

Benefits:

In addition to being a fantastic source of calcium, protein, and antioxidants to promote bone health and immune function, savory Parmesan and herb overnight oats provide rich and tasty taste experience with a combination of tangy Parmesan cheese and fragrant herbs.

Asian-inspired Sesame Ginger Overnight Oats

Ingredients:

♡ 1/2 cup rolled oats
♡ 1/2 cup vegetable broth
♡ 1/4 cup Greek yogurt
♡ One tablespoon of soy sauce
♡ One tablespoon of rice vinegar
♡ One teaspoon of sesame oil
♡ 1/2 teaspoon grated ginger
♡ One tablespoon of chopped green onions
♡ One tablespoon toasted sesame seeds

Directions:

⚡ Place the veggie broth and rolled oats in a jar or dish.
⚡ Add the toasted sesame seeds, Greek yogurt, soy sauc rice vinegar, sesame oil, grated ginger, and sliced green onions.

⚡ Refrigerate overnight with a cover on.
⚡ Stir the oats and adjust the seasoning if necessary in the morning.
⚡ As desired, serve warm or cold.

Benefits:
Asian-inspired sesame ginger overnight oats are a great source of protein, healthy fats, and vital nutrients to promote heart health and brain function. They have a savory and aromatic taste profile with a hint of umami from soy sauce and sesame oil.

Caprese Overnight Oats with Tomato and Basil

Ingredients:
♡ 1/2 cup rolled oats
♡ 1/2 cup vegetable broth
♡ 1/4 cup Greek yogurt
♡ 1/4 cup diced tomatoes
♡ Two tablespoons chopped fresh basil
♡ One tablespoon of balsamic vinegar
♡ One tablespoon of olive oil
♡ Salt and pepper to taste
♡ Mozzarella cheese for garnish (optional)

Directions:
⚡ Place the veggie broth and rolled oats in a jar or dish.
⚡ Add the Greek yogurt, chopped fresh basil, diced tomatoes, olive oil, balsamic vinegar, and salt and pepper to taste.
⚡ Refrigerate overnight with a cover on.
⚡ Stir the oats and adjust the seasoning if necessary in the morning.
⚡ Serve warm or cold, with the option to add mozzarella cheese as a garnish.

Benefits:

With their typical tomato, basil, and balsamic vinegar flavor, caprese overnight oats are a refreshing and flavorful breakfast option. They are also an excellent source of antioxidants, healthy fats, and vital nutrients that boost immune system function and encourage fullness throughout the morning.

Curry Spiced Savory Oats with Chickpeas

Ingredients:

- ♡ 1/2 cup rolled oats
- ♡ 1/2 cup vegetable broth
- ♡ 1/4 cup Greek yogurt
- ♡ 1/4 cup cooked chickpeas
- ♡ One tablespoon of curry powder
- ♡ 1/2 teaspoon ground turmeric
- ♡ 1/4 teaspoon ground cumin
- ♡ 1/4 teaspoon ground coriander
- ♡ Salt and pepper to taste
- ♡ Chopped cilantro for garnish (optional)

Directions:

⚡ Place the veggie broth and rolled oats in a jar or dish.

⚡ Add the cooked chickpeas, Greek yogurt, curry powder, turmeric, cumin, coriander, salt, and pepper and stir.

⚡ Refrigerate overnight with a cover on.

⚡ Stir the oats and adjust the seasoning if necessary in the morning.

⚡ Serve warm or cold, with chopped cilantro on top if you'd like.

Benefits:

With a combination of creamy chickpeas and curry spices, these savory oats with chickpeas have a strong and fragrant taste profile. They're also a fantastic source of plant-based protein, fiber, and anti-inflammatory components to promote intestinal health and well-being.

Savory Mushroom and Spinach Overnight Oats

Ingredients:

- ♡ 1/2 cup rolled oats
- ♡ 1/2 cup vegetable broth
- ♡ 1/4 cup Greek yogurt
- ♡ 1/4 cup sliced mushrooms
- ♡ 1/2 cup fresh spinach leaves
- ♡ One tablespoon chopped onion
- ♡ One clove of garlic, minced
- ♡ Salt and pepper to taste
- ♡ Grated Parmesan cheese, for garnish (optional)

Directions:

⚡ Place the veggie broth and rolled oats in a jar or dish.

⚡ Add Greek yogurt, chopped onion, minced garlic, fresh spinach leaves, sliced mushrooms, and salt and pepper to taste.

⚡ Refrigerate overnight with a cover on.

⚡ Stir the oats and adjust the seasoning if necessary in the morning.

⚡ Serve warm or cold, topped with grated Parmesan cheese, if preferred.

Benefits:

With earthy mushrooms, soft spinach, and fragrant garlic, savory mushrooms, and spinach overnight oats provide a satisfying and nourishing breakfast choice. They are also a rich source of vitamins, minerals, and antioxidants to boost immune function and encourage fullness throughout the morning.

Greek Salad Inspired Overnight Oats

Ingredients:
- ♡ 1/2 cup rolled oats
- ♡ 1/2 cup vegetable broth
- ♡ 1/4 cup Greek yogurt
- ♡ 1/4 cup diced cucumber
- ♡ 1/4 cup diced tomato
- ♡ 1/4 cup diced bell pepper
- ♡ Two tablespoons chopped red onion
- ♡ Two tablespoons of crumbled feta cheese
- ♡ One tablespoon chopped Kalamata olives
- ♡ One tablespoon of chopped fresh parsley
- ♡ Salt and pepper to taste

Directions:
- ⚡ Place the veggie broth and rolled oats in a jar or dish.
- ⚡ Add the Greek yogurt, chopped fresh parsley, Kalamata olives, tomatoes, bell pepper, cucumber, red onion, and crumbled feta cheese.
- ⚡ Refrigerate overnight with a cover on.
- ⚡ Stir the oats and adjust the seasoning if necessary in the morning.
- ⚡ As desired, serve warm or cold.

Benefits:

Inspired by a Greek salad, these overnight oats are a light and nourishing breakfast choice. Topped with tart feta cheese, crisp veggies, and flavorful olives, they're high in fiber, vitamins, and minerals that promote healthy digestion and well-being.

Ratatouille Overnight Oats with Eggplant and Zucchini

Ingredients:

- ♡ 1/2 cup rolled oats
- ♡ 1/2 cup vegetable broth
- ♡ 1/4 cup Greek yogurt
- ♡ 1/4 cup diced eggplant
- ♡ 1/4 cup diced zucchini
- ♡ 1/4 cup diced bell pepper
- ♡ Two tablespoons diced onion
- ♡ One clove of garlic, minced
- ♡ Two tablespoons of tomato sauce
- ♡ 1/2 teaspoon dried thyme
- ♡ Salt and pepper to taste
- ♡ Fresh basil, for garnish (optional)

Directions:

⚡ Place the veggie broth and rolled oats in a jar or dish.
⚡ Add the Greek yogurt, chopped bell pepper, chopped onion, chopped eggplant, chopped zucchini, minced garlic, tomato sauce, dried thyme, salt, and pepper.
⚡ Refrigerate overnight with a cover on.
⚡ Stir the oats and adjust the seasoning if necessary in the morning.
Garnish with fresh basil and serve warm or cold as preferred.

Benefits:

Inspired by the traditional French dish, ratatouille overnight oats are a tasty and filling breakfast alternative. They are high in fiber, antioxidants, and vitamins that support heart health and encourage satiety throughout the morning.

Smoky BBQ Overnight Oats with Tempeh Bits

Ingredients:

♡ 1/2 cup rolled oats
♡ 1/2 cup vegetable broth
♡ 1/4 cup Greek yogurt
♡ Two tablespoons of barbecue sauce
♡ Two tablespoons diced tempeh
♡ One tablespoon diced red onion
♡ One tablespoon of diced bell pepper
♡ 1/2 teaspoon smoked paprika
♡ Salt and pepper to taste
♡ Fresh cilantro for garnish (optional)

Directions:

⚡ Place the veggie broth and rolled oats in a jar or dish.
⚡ Add Greek yogurt, smoked paprika, bell pepper, red onion, tempeh, and barbecue sauce. Mix well.
⚡ Refrigerate overnight with a cover on.
⚡ Stir the oats and adjust the seasoning if necessary in the morning.
⚡ Serve warm or cold, with fresh cilantro on top if preferred

Benefits:

With their robust barbecue flavor and hearty tempeh, Smoky BBQ overnight oats with tempeh bits make a savory and filling breakfast option. They also serve as a good source of plant-based protein, fiber, and vital nutrients to support muscle repair and recovery and promote sustained energy throughout the morning.

Vegan Overnight Oats Recipes

Peanut Butter Chocolate Chip Vegan Overnight Oats

Ingredients:
- ♡ 1/2 cup rolled oats
- ♡ 1/2 cup almond milk (or any plant-based milk)
- ♡ Two tablespoons of peanut butter
- ♡ One tablespoon of maple syrup
- ♡ One tablespoon of vegan chocolate chips
- ♡ 1/2 teaspoon vanilla extract

Directions:
- ⚡ Rolling oats, almond milk, peanut butter, maple syrup, vegan chocolate chips, and vanilla essence should all be combined in a dish or container.
- ⚡ Mix well to blend.
- ⚡ Refrigerate overnight with a cover on.
- ⚡ Stir the oats and adjust the sweetness if necessary in the morning.
- ⚡ As desired, serve warm or cold.

Benefits:
A fantastic source of protein, healthy fats, and antioxidants to support heart health and promote satiety throughout the morning, peanut butter chocolate chip vegan overnight oats have a creamy and decadent taste that perfectly combines peanut butter and chocolate.

Mixed Berry Coconut Vegan Overnight Oats

Ingredients:
- ♡ 1/2 cup rolled oats
- ♡ 1/2 cup coconut milk (or any plant-based milk)
- ♡ 1/4 cup mixed berries (strawberries, blueberries, raspberries)
- ♡ Two tablespoons shredded coconut

♡ One tablespoon of maple syrup or agave syrup
♡ 1/2 teaspoon vanilla extract

Directions:

⚡ Rolling oats, coconut milk, mixed berries, shredded coconut, maple syrup, and vanilla essence should all be combined in a dish or container.
⚡ Mix well to blend.
⚡ Refrigerate overnight with a cover on.
⚡ Stir the oats and adjust the sweetness if necessary in the morning.
⚡ As desired, serve warm or cold.

Benefits:

With a tropical coconut taste, mixed berry coconut vegan overnight oats are tasty and refreshing. They are also an excellent source of fiber, vitamins, and minerals that support digestive health and enhance general well-being.

Mango Turmeric Vegan Overnight Oats

Ingredients:

♡ 1/2 cup rolled oats
♡ 1/2 cup coconut milk (or any plant-based milk)
♡ 1/4 cup diced mango
♡ One tablespoon of chia seeds
♡ One tablespoon of maple syrup or agave syrup
♡ 1/2 teaspoon ground turmeric
♡ Pinch of black pepper (to enhance turmeric absorption)
♡ 1/2 teaspoon vanilla extract

Directions:

⚡ Rolling oats, coconut milk, sliced mango, chia seeds, maple syrup, ground turmeric, black pepper, and vanilla essence should all be combined in a dish or container.
⚡ Mix well to blend.
⚡ Refrigerate overnight with a cover on.

⚡ Stir the oats and adjust the sweetness if necessary in the morning.
⚡ As desired, serve warm or cold.

Benefits:
Turmeric's anti-inflammatory properties and mango's sweetness give these vegan overnight oats a tropical touch. They're also an excellent source of fiber, antioxidants, and other vital nutrients that boost immune function and reduce inflammation.

Almond Joy Vegan Overnight Oats

Ingredients:
♡ 1/2 cup rolled oats
♡ 1/2 cup almond milk (or any plant-based milk)
♡ Two tablespoons shredded coconut
♡ One tablespoon of cocoa powder
♡ One tablespoon of maple syrup or agave syrup
♡ One tablespoon of sliced almonds

Directions:
⚡ Rolling oats, almond milk, shredded coconut, cocoa powder, maple syrup, and sliced almonds should all be combined in a dish or container.
⚡ Mix well to blend.
⚡ Refrigerate overnight with a cover on.
⚡ Stir the oats and adjust the sweetness if necessary in the morning.
⚡ As desired, serve warm or cold.

Benefits:
With a rich and fulfilling taste evocative of the beloved candy bar, Almond Joy vegan overnight oats are a great source of heart-healthy fats, antioxidants, and fiber that help with satiety all morning long.

Pumpkin Spice Vegan Overnight Oats

Ingredients:

- ♡ 1/2 cup rolled oats
- ♡ 1/2 cup almond milk (or any plant-based milk)
- ♡ 1/4 cup pumpkin puree
- ♡ One tablespoon of maple syrup or agave syrup
- ♡ 1/2 teaspoon pumpkin pie spice
- ♡ 1/2 teaspoon vanilla extract

Directions:

⚡ Mix the rolling oats, almond milk, pureed pumpkin, maple syrup, pumpkin pie spice, and vanilla essence in a plate or container.

⚡ To blend, thoroughly mix.

⚡ Cover and refrigerate overnight.

⚡ In the morning, stir the oats and adjust the sweetness if needed.

⚡ Serve warm or cold as preferred.

Benefits:

With the natural sweetness of pumpkin and toasty spices, pumpkin spice vegan overnight oats provide the cozy taste of autumn. They're also an excellent source of fiber, vitamins, and antioxidants to support digestive health and enhance general well-being.

Chocolate Raspberry Chia Vegan Overnight Oats

Ingredients:

- ♡ 1/2 cup rolled oats
- ♡ 1/2 cup almond milk (or any plant-based milk)
- ♡ 1/4 cup raspberries
- ♡ One tablespoon of chia seeds
- ♡ One tablespoon of cocoa powder
- ♡ One tablespoon of maple syrup or agave syrup

Directions:
⚡ Rolling oats, almond milk, chia seeds, raspberries, cocoa powder, and maple syrup should all be combined in a dish or container.

⚡ Mix well to blend.

⚡ Refrigerate overnight with a cover on.

⚡ Stir the oats and adjust the sweetness if necessary in the morning.

⚡ As desired, serve warm or cold.

Benefits:
Rich chocolate taste and tart raspberries combine in these delicious vegan overnight oats. They are also an excellent source of fiber, antioxidants, and vital minerals that support heart health and encourage fullness throughout the morning.

Matcha Green Tea Vegan Overnight Oats

Ingredients:
♡ 1/2 cup rolled oats

♡ 1/2 cup almond milk (or any plant-based milk)

♡ One tablespoon of matcha powder

♡ One tablespoon of maple syrup or agave syrup

♡ 1/2 teaspoon vanilla extract

Directions:
⚡ Combine rolling oats, almond milk, matcha powder, maple syrup, and vanilla essence in a basin or container.

⚡ Mix well to blend.

⚡ Refrigerate overnight with a cover on.

⚡ Stir the oats and adjust the sweetness if necessary in the morning.

⚡ As desired, serve warm or cold.

Benefits:
Matcha green tea vegan overnight oats have a distinct and refreshing taste thanks to their nutritional advantages. They are a substantial source of antioxidants, vitamins, and amir acids that boost attention, concentration, and general well-being.

Vanilla Almond Vegan Overnight Oats

Ingredients:
- ♡ 1/2 cup rolled oats
- ♡ 1/2 cup almond milk (or any plant-based milk)
- ♡ One tablespoon of almond butter
- ♡ One tablespoon of maple syrup or agave syrup
- ♡ 1/2 teaspoon vanilla extract
- ♡ Sliced almonds for garnish (optional)

Directions:
⚡ Rolling oats, almond milk, almond butter, maple syrup, and vanilla extract should all be combined in a dish or container.
⚡ Mix well to blend.
⚡ Refrigerate overnight with a cover on.
⚡ Stir the oats and adjust the sweetness if necessary in th morning.
⚡ Serve warm or cold, with sliced almonds on top if preferred.

Benefits:
With the natural sweetness of almond butter and vanilla, vanilla almond vegan overnight oats provide a satisfying a nutritious breakfast alternative. They are also a fantastic source of protein, healthy fats, and vital nutrients to mainte energy levels and encourage satiety throughout the mornir

Pineapple Coconut Vegan Overnight Oats

Ingredients:
- ♡ 1/2 cup rolled oats
- ♡ 1/2 cup coconut milk (or any plant-based milk)
- ♡ 1/4 cup diced pineapple
- ♡ Two tablespoons shredded coconut
- ♡ One tablespoon of maple syrup or agave syrup
- ♡ 1/2 teaspoon vanilla extract

Directions:
⚡ Rolling oats, coconut milk, sliced pineapple, shredded coconut, maple syrup, and vanilla essence should all be combined in a dish or container.
⚡ Mix well to blend.
⚡ Refrigerate overnight with a cover on.
⚡ Stir the oats and adjust the sweetness if necessary in the morning.
⚡ As desired, serve warm or cold.

Benefits:
With the sweetness of pineapple and the richness of coconut, pineapple coconut vegan overnight oats provide a taste of the tropics while also serving as a healthy source of fiber, vitamins, and minerals to aid digestion and enhance general well-being.

Blueberry Banana Vegan Overnight Oats

Ingredients:
- ♡ 1/2 cup rolled oats
- ♡ 1/2 cup almond milk (or any plant-based milk)
- ♡ 1/4 cup blueberries
- ♡ 1/2 ripe banana, mashed
- ♡ One tablespoon of maple syrup or agave syrup
- ♡ 1/2 teaspoon vanilla extract

Directions:

⚡ Rolling oats, almond milk, blueberries, mashed banana, maple syrup, and vanilla essence should all be combined in a dish or container.

⚡ Mix well to blend.

⚡ Refrigerate overnight with a cover on.

⚡ Stir the oats and adjust the sweetness if necessary in the morning.

⚡ As desired, serve warm or cold.

Benefits:

With the natural sweetness of bananas and the antioxidant-rich blueberries, blueberry banana vegan overnight oats have a pleasant and delicious taste. They are also an excellent dose of fiber, vitamins, and minerals to support digestive health and encourage fullness throughout the morning.

Gluten-Free Overnight Oats Recipes

Classic Gluten-Free Overnight Oats

Ingredients:
- ♡ 1/2 cup gluten-free rolled oats
- ♡ 1/2 cup almond milk (or any preferred milk)
- ♡ One tablespoon of maple syrup or honey (optional)
- ♡ 1/2 teaspoon vanilla extract
- ♡ Pinch of salt

Directions:
- ⚡ Almond milk, rolled oats, salt, vanilla extract, and maple syrup (if used) should all be combined in a dish or jar.
- ⚡ Mix well to blend.
- ⚡ Refrigerate overnight with a cover on.
- ⚡ Stir the oats and adjust the sweetness if necessary in the morning.
- ⚡ As desired, serve warm or cold.

Benefits:
With maple syrup's natural sweetness and creamy texture, classic gluten-free overnight oats provide a quick and filling breakfast choice. They are also an excellent source of fiber, vitamins, and minerals to support digestive health and encourage fullness throughout the morning.

Gluten-Free Apple Pie Overnight Oats

Ingredients:
- ♡ 1/2 cup gluten-free rolled oats
- ♡ 1/2 cup almond milk (or any preferred milk)
- ♡ 1/4 cup diced apple
- ♡ One tablespoon of maple syrup or honey
- ♡ 1/4 teaspoon ground cinnamon
- ♡ Pinch of nutmeg
- ♡ Pinch of salt

Directions:

⚡ Rolling oats, almond milk, sliced apple, maple syrup, nutmeg, ground cinnamon, and salt should all be combined in a dish or container.

⚡ Mix well to blend.

⚡ Refrigerate overnight with a cover on.

⚡ Stir the oats and adjust the sweetness if necessary in the morning.

⚡ As desired, serve warm or cold.

Benefits:

Apple pie without gluten Overnight oats combine the soothing aromas of apple pie with the health benefits of oats. They are high in fiber, antioxidants, and vital minerals that support heart health and encourage fullness throughout the morning.

Gluten-Free Lemon Poppy Seed Overnight Oats

Ingredients:

♡ 1/2 cup gluten-free rolled oats
♡ 1/2 cup almond milk (or any preferred milk)
♡ One tablespoon of maple syrup or honey
♡ Zest of 1 lemon
♡ One tablespoon of lemon juice
♡ One teaspoon of poppy seeds
♡ Pinch of salt

Directions:

⚡ Combine rolling oats, almond milk, maple syrup, lemon zest and juice, poppy seeds, and salt in a dish or container.

⚡ Mix well to blend.

⚡ Refrigerate overnight with a cover on.

⚡ Stir the oats and adjust the sweetness if necessary in the morning.

⚡ As desired, serve warm or cold.

Benefits:
With a beautiful crunch from the poppy seeds and a crisp and tangy taste, gluten-free lemon poppy seed overnight oats are a great source of antioxidants, vitamin C, and other vital nutrients that support immune health and encourage satiety throughout the morning.

Gluten-Free Cherry Almond Overnight Oats

Ingredients:
♡ 1/2 cup gluten-free rolled oats
♡ 1/2 cup almond milk (or any preferred milk)
♡ 1/4 cup cherries, pitted and halved
♡ One tablespoon of maple syrup or honey
♡ One tablespoon of almond butter
♡ One tablespoon of sliced almonds
♡ Pinch of salt

Directions:
⚡ Rolling oats, almond milk, cherries, maple syrup, almond butter, sliced almonds, and salt should all be combined in a dish or container.
⚡ Mix well to blend.
⚡ Refrigerate overnight with a cover on.
⚡ Stir the oats and adjust the sweetness if necessary in the morning.
⚡ As desired, serve warm or cold.

Benefits:
The lovely mix of sweet cherries, nutty almonds, and creamy almond butter found in gluten-free cherry almond overnight oats is sure to please. They are also a fantastic source of antioxidants, healthy fats, and vital nutrients that support heart health and encourage satiety throughout the morning.

Gluten-Free Carrot Cake Overnight Oats

Ingredients:
- ♡ 1/2 cup gluten-free rolled oats
- ♡ 1/2 cup almond milk (or any preferred milk)
- ♡ 1/4 cup grated carrot
- ♡ Two tablespoons chopped walnuts
- ♡ One tablespoon of maple syrup or honey
- ♡ 1/2 teaspoon ground cinnamon
- ♡ 1/4 teaspoon ground nutmeg
- ♡ Pinch of salt

Directions:
⚡ Rolling oats, almond milk, shredded carrot, chopped walnuts, maple syrup, ground nutmeg, ground cinnamon, and salt should all be combined in a dish or container.
⚡ Mix well to blend.
⚡ Refrigerate overnight with a cover on.
⚡ Stir the oats and adjust the sweetness if necessary in th morning.
⚡ As desired, serve warm or cold.

Benefits:
Carrot cake overnight oats without gluten provide the famil aromas of carrot cake in a healthy breakfast alternative. Th are high in fiber, beta-carotene, and other essential nutrien that support eye health and encourage satiety throughout t morning.

Gluten-Free Pina Colada Overnight Oats

Ingredients:
- ♡ 1/2 cup gluten-free rolled oats
- ♡ 1/2 cup coconut milk (or any preferred milk)
- ♡ 1/4 cup diced pineapple
- ♡ Two tablespoons shredded coconut
- ♡ One tablespoon of maple syrup or honey

♡ 1/4 teaspoon vanilla extract

Directions:
⚡ Rolling oats, coconut milk, sliced pineapple, shredded coconut, maple syrup, and vanilla essence should all be combined in a dish or container.
⚡ Mix well to blend.
⚡ Refrigerate overnight with a cover on.
⚡ Stir the oats and adjust the sweetness if necessary in the morning.
⚡ As desired, serve warm or cold.

Benefits:
With the sweetness of pineapple and the creaminess of coconut, gluten-free pina colada overnight oats provide a taste of the tropics while also serving as a rich source of fiber, vitamins, and minerals to support digestive health and improve general well-being.

Gluten-Free Chocolate Hazelnut Overnight Oats

Ingredients:
♡ 1/2 cup gluten-free rolled oats
♡ 1/2 cup almond milk (or any preferred milk)
♡ One tablespoon of cocoa powder
♡ One tablespoon of hazelnut butter
♡ One tablespoon of maple syrup or honey
♡ One tablespoon chopped hazelnuts
♡ Pinch of salt

Directions:
⚡ Almond milk, cocoa powder, hazelnut butter, maple syrup, chopped hazelnuts, and salt should all be combined with rolled oats in a bowl or container.
⚡ Mix well to blend.
⚡ Refrigerate overnight with a cover on.

⚡ Stir the oats and adjust the sweetness if necessary in the morning.

⚡ As desired, serve warm or cold.

Benefits:

Rich in chocolate and creamy hazelnut, gluten-free chocolate hazelnut overnight oats are a rich-tasting treat packed with heart-healthy fats, antioxidants, and vital nutrients that help you feel full all morning.

Gluten-Free Banana Bread Overnight Oats

Ingredients:

♡ 1/2 cup gluten-free rolled oats
♡ 1/2 cup almond milk (or any preferred milk)
♡ 1/2 ripe banana, mashed
♡ One tablespoon of maple syrup or honey
♡ One tablespoon of chopped walnuts
♡ 1/2 teaspoon ground cinnamon
♡ Pinch of salt

Directions:

⚡ Combine rolling oats, almond milk, mashed banana, maple syrup, chopped walnuts, ground cinnamon, and salt in a dish or container.

⚡ Mix well to blend.

⚡ Refrigerate overnight with a cover on.

⚡ Stir the oats and adjust the sweetness if necessary in the morning.

⚡ As desired, serve warm or cold.

Benefits:

The familiar aromas of banana bread are available in gluten-free banana bread overnight oats, which also serve as a healthy breakfast alternative. They are a rich source of potassium, fiber, and other nutrients that support heart health and encourage satiety throughout the morning.

Gluten-Free Maple Walnut Overnight Oats

Ingredients:
♡ 1/2 cup gluten-free rolled oats
♡ 1/2 cup almond milk (or any preferred milk)
♡ One tablespoon of maple syrup
♡ One tablespoon of chopped walnuts
♡ 1/4 teaspoon ground cinnamon
♡ Pinch of salt

Directions:
⚡ Combine rolling oats, almond milk, maple syrup, chopped walnuts, ground cinnamon, and salt in a dish or container.
⚡ Mix well to blend.
⚡ Refrigerate overnight with a cover on.
⚡ Stir the oats and adjust the sweetness if necessary in the morning.
⚡ As desired, serve warm or cold.

Benefits:
With a soothing and nutty taste enhanced by the sweetness of maple syrup, gluten-free maple walnut overnight oats are a great source of antioxidants, omega-3 fatty acids, and other vital nutrients that support brain health and encourage satiety throughout the morning.

Gluten-Free Peach Cobbler Overnight Oats

Ingredients:
♡ 1/2 cup gluten-free rolled oats
♡ 1/2 cup almond milk (or any preferred milk)
♡ 1/4 cup diced peaches
♡ One tablespoon of maple syrup
♡ One tablespoon of chopped pecans
♡ 1/4 teaspoon ground cinnamon
♡ Pinch of nutmeg
♡ Pinch of salt

Directions:

⚡ Rolling oats, almond milk, sliced peaches, chopped pecans, maple syrup, nutmeg, and salt should all be combined in a dish or container.

⚡ Mix well to blend.

⚡ Refrigerate overnight with a cover on.

⚡ Stir the oats and adjust the sweetness if necessary in the morning.

⚡ As desired, serve warm or cold.

Benefits:

With a soothing taste of nutmeg and cinnamon and a delightfully sweet and fruity flavor, gluten-free peach cobbler overnight oats are an excellent source of fiber, vitamins, and antioxidants to support digestive health and improve overall well-being.

Nut Butter Lover's Overnight Oats

Peanut Butter Banana Overnight Oats

Ingredients:
- ♡ 1/2 cup rolled oats
- ♡ 1/2 cup almond milk (or any preferred milk)
- ♡ 1/2 ripe banana, mashed
- ♡ One tablespoon of peanut butter
- ♡ One tablespoon of maple syrup or honey (optional)
- ♡ Pinch of salt

Directions:
- ⚡ Combine rolling oats, almond milk, mashed banana, peanut butter, maple syrup (if used), and salt in a bowl or container.
- ⚡ Mix well to blend.
- ⚡ Refrigerate overnight with a cover on.
- ⚡ Stir the oats and adjust the sweetness if necessary in the morning.
- ⚡ As desired, serve warm or cold.

Benefits:
With the natural sweetness of bananas and the nutty taste of peanut butter, peanut butter banana overnight oats have a traditional and cozy flavor. They also serve as an excellent source of protein, healthy fats, and vital nutrients to enhance energy levels and encourage satiety throughout the morning.

Almond Butter and Jelly Overnight Oats

Ingredients:
- ♡ 1/2 cup rolled oats
- ♡ 1/2 cup almond milk (or any preferred milk)
- ♡ One tablespoon of almond butter
- ♡ Two tablespoons of fruit jam or jelly (any preferred flavor)
- ♡ One tablespoon of maple syrup or honey (optional)

♡ Pinch of salt

Directions:

⚡ Rolling oats, almond milk, almond butter, fruit jam or jell maple syrup (if used), and salt should all be combined in a dish or container.
⚡ Mix well to blend.
⚡ Refrigerate overnight with a cover on.
⚡ Stir the oats and adjust the sweetness if necessary in th morning.
⚡ As desired, serve warm or cold.

Benefits:

Almond butter and jelly overnight oats are a great source o heart-healthy fats, antioxidants, and vital nutrients that support heart health and encourage satiety throughout the morning. They also have a nostalgic and sweet taste that brings back memories of childhood favorite sandwiches.

Cashew Butter Chocolate Chip Overnight Oats

Ingredients:

♡ 1/2 cup rolled oats
♡ 1/2 cup almond milk (or any preferred milk)
♡ One tablespoon of cashew butter
♡ One tablespoon of maple syrup or honey (optional)
♡ One tablespoon of chocolate chips
♡ Pinch of salt

Directions:

⚡ Almond milk, cashew butter, chocolate chips, salt, and maple syrup (if used) should all be combined with rolled oa in a bowl or jar.
⚡ Mix well to blend.
⚡ Refrigerate overnight with a cover on.

⚡ Stir the oats and adjust the sweetness if necessary in the morning.
⚡ As desired, serve warm or cold.

Benefits:
Chocolate chips with cashew butter: With their rich chocolate and creamy butter flavor, overnight oats are a rich and delectable breakfast option. They are also a fantastic source of protein, healthy fats, and antioxidants, improving energy levels and encouraging fullness throughout the morning.

Hazelnut Butter and Berry Overnight Oats

Ingredients:
♡ 1/2 cup rolled oats
♡ 1/2 cup almond milk (or any preferred milk)
♡ One tablespoon of hazelnut butter
♡ One tablespoon of maple syrup or honey (optional)
♡ 1/4 cup mixed berries (strawberries, blueberries, raspberries)
♡ Pinch of salt

Directions:
⚡ Rolling oats, almond milk, hazelnut butter, maple syrup (if used), mixed berries, and salt should all be combined in a bowl or container.
⚡ Mix well to blend.
⚡ Refrigerate overnight with a cover on.
⚡ Stir the oats and adjust the sweetness if necessary in the morning.
⚡ As desired, serve warm or cold.

Benefits:
Overnight oats with hazelnut butter and berries are a delicious blend of creamy hazelnut taste and tart berries. They are also an excellent source of fiber, antioxidants, and other vital nutrients that support overall health and encourage fullness throughout the morning.

Sunflower Seed Butter Maple Overnight Oats

Ingredients:
♡ 1/2 cup rolled oats
♡ 1/2 cup almond milk (or any preferred milk)
♡ One tablespoon of sunflower seed butter
♡ One tablespoon of maple syrup
♡ Pinch of salt

Directions:
⚡ Rolling oats, almond milk, sunflower seed butter, maple syrup, and salt should all be combined in a dish or container.
⚡ Mix well to blend.
⚡ Refrigerate overnight with a cover on.
⚡ Stir the oats and adjust the sweetness if necessary in the morning.
⚡ As desired, serve warm or cold.

Benefits:
In addition to having a distinctive, nutty taste enhanced by the sweetness of maple syrup, sunflower seed butter maple overnight oats are a great source of protein, healthy fats, and vital elements that help sustain energy levels and encourage fullness throughout the morning.

Pistachio Butter and Fig Overnight Oats

Ingredients:
♡ 1/2 cup rolled oats
♡ 1/2 cup almond milk (or any preferred milk)
♡ One tablespoon of pistachio butter
♡ One tablespoon of maple syrup or honey
♡ 2-3 dried figs, chopped
♡ Pinch of salt

Directions:
⚡ Rolling oats, almond milk, pistachio butter, maple syrup (or honey), chopped dried figs, and salt should all be combined in a dish or container.
⚡ Mix well to blend.
⚡ Refrigerate overnight with a cover on.
⚡ Stir the oats and adjust the sweetness if necessary in the morning.
⚡ As desired, serve warm or cold.

Benefits:
The nuttiness of pistachios and the inherent sweetness of figs, pistachio butter, and fig overnight oats provide a distinctive and tasty combination. They also serve as a healthy source of fiber, antioxidants, and vital nutrients that support heart health and encourage satiety throughout the morning.

Macadamia Nut Butter and Pineapple Overnight Oats

Ingredients:
♡ 1/2 cup rolled oats
♡ 1/2 cup coconut milk (or any preferred milk)
♡ One tablespoon of macadamia nut butter
♡ One tablespoon of maple syrup or honey
♡ 1/4 cup diced pineapple
♡ Pinch of salt

Directions:
⚡ Combine rolling oats, coconut milk, macadamia nut butter, sliced pineapple, maple syrup (or honey), and salt in a dish or container.
⚡ Mix well to blend.
⚡ Refrigerate overnight with a cover on.
⚡ Stir the oats and adjust the sweetness if necessary in the morning.
⚡ As desired, serve warm or cold.

Benefits:

With the creamy texture of macadamia nuts and the sweetness of pineapple, macadamia nut butter, and pineapple overnight oats have a tropical and decadent taste. They are also an excellent source of healthy fats, vitamins, and minerals to support overall well-being and encourage satiety throughout the morning.

Walnut Butter and Apple Overnight Oats

Ingredients:

- ♡ 1/2 cup rolled oats
- ♡ 1/2 cup almond milk (or any preferred milk)
- ♡ One tablespoon of walnut butter
- ♡ One tablespoon of maple syrup or honey
- ♡ 1/4 cup diced apple
- ♡ Pinch of cinnamon
- ♡ Pinch of salt

Directions:

⚡ Rolling oats, almond milk, walnut butter, maple syrup (or honey), chopped apple, cinnamon, and salt should all be combined in a dish or container.

⚡ Mix well to blend.

⚡ Refrigerate overnight with a cover on.

⚡ Stir the oats and adjust the sweetness if necessary in the morning.

⚡ As desired, serve warm or cold.

Benefits:

In addition to being a healthy source of antioxidants, fiber, and vital minerals to support heart health and promote satiety throughout the morning, walnut butter and apple overnight oats have a pleasant and nutty taste enhanced by the sweetness of the apple and the richness of the walnuts.

Pecan Butter and Maple Overnight Oats

Ingredients:
- ♡ 1/2 cup rolled oats
- ♡ 1/2 cup almond milk (or any preferred milk)
- ♡ One tablespoon of pecan butter
- ♡ One tablespoon of maple syrup
- ♡ One tablespoon of chopped pecans
- ♡ Pinch of salt

Directions:
⚡ Rolling oats, almond milk, pecan butter, maple syrup, chopped nuts, and salt should all be combined in a basin or container.
⚡ Mix well to blend.
⚡ Refrigerate overnight with a cover on.
⚡ Stir the oats and adjust the sweetness if necessary in the morning.
⚡ As desired, serve warm or cold.

Benefits:
Rich and nutty in taste, pecan butter and maple overnight oats pair well with maple syrup's sweetness. They are also an excellent source of essential nutrients, healthy fats, and antioxidants that support brain health and encourage satiety throughout the morning.

Coconut Cashew Butter Overnight Oats

Ingredients:
- ♡ 1/2 cup rolled oats
- ♡ 1/2 cup coconut milk (or any preferred milk)
- ♡ One tablespoon of cashew butter
- ♡ One tablespoon of shredded coconut
- ♡ One tablespoon of maple syrup or honey
- ♡ Pinch of salt

Directions:

⚡ Rolling oats, coconut milk, cashew butter, shredded coconut, maple syrup (or honey), and salt should all be combined in a dish or container.

⚡ Mix well to blend.

⚡ Refrigerate overnight with a cover on.

⚡ Stir the oats and adjust the sweetness if necessary in the morning.

⚡ As desired, serve warm or cold.

Benefits:

With the richness of cashew butter and the sweetness of coconut, coconut cashew butter overnight oats have a creamy, tropical taste. They are also an excellent source of protein, healthy fats, and vital nutrients to maintain energy levels and encourage satiety throughout the morning.

Seasonal Overnight Oats Recipes

Spiced Pumpkin Pie Overnight Oats

Ingredients:
- ♡ 1/2 cup rolled oats
- ♡ 1/2 cup almond milk (or any preferred milk)
- ♡ 1/4 cup pumpkin puree
- ♡ One tablespoon of maple syrup
- ♡ 1/2 teaspoon pumpkin pie spice (or a mix of cinnamon, nutmeg, and cloves)
- ♡ Pinch of salt

Directions:
⚡ Almond milk, pumpkin puree, maple syrup, pumpkin pie spice, and salt should all be combined with rolled oats in a bowl or container.
⚡ Mix well to blend.
⚡ Refrigerate overnight with a cover on.
⚡ Stir the oats and adjust the sweetness if necessary in the morning.
⚡ As desired, serve warm or cold.

Benefits:
With the richness of pumpkin and warming spices, spiced pumpkin pie overnight oats give a cozy and seasonal taste. They're also an excellent source of fiber, antioxidants, and vital minerals to support immune health and encourage satiety throughout the morning.

Cranberry Orange Overnight Oats

Ingredients:
- ♡ 1/2 cup rolled oats
- ♡ 1/2 cup almond milk (or any preferred milk)
- ♡ 1/4 cup dried cranberries
- ♡ Zest of 1 orange

♡ One tablespoon of maple syrup or honey
♡ Pinch of salt

Directions:

⚡ Rolling oats, almond milk, orange zest, dried cranberries, maple syrup (or honey), and salt should all be combined in a dish or container.
⚡ Mix well to blend.
⚡ Refrigerate overnight with a cover on.
⚡ Stir the oats and adjust the sweetness if necessary in the morning.
⚡ As desired, serve warm or cold.

Benefits:

Cranberry orange overnight oats are a great source of vitamin C, antioxidants, and other vital nutrients to support immune health and encourage satiety throughout the morning. They have a tangy, citrusy taste with a sweetness from the cranberries.

Apple Cider Overnight Oats

Ingredients:

♡ 1/2 cup rolled oats
♡ 1/2 cup apple cider
♡ 1/4 cup unsweetened applesauce
♡ One tablespoon of maple syrup or honey
♡ 1/2 teaspoon ground cinnamon
♡ Pinch of salt

Directions:

⚡ Rolling oats, apple cider, applesauce, maple syrup (or honey), ground cinnamon, and salt should all be combined in a bowl or container.
⚡ Mix well to blend.
⚡ Refrigerate overnight with a cover on.

⚡ Stir the oats and adjust the sweetness if necessary in the morning.
⚡ As desired, serve warm or cold.

Benefits:
With the sweetness of apple cider and the warmth of cinnamon, apple cider overnight oats have a delightful fall taste. They are also an excellent source of fiber, vitamins, and antioxidants to support digestive health and encourage fullness throughout the morning.

Gingerbread Overnight Oats

Ingredients:
♡ 1/2 cup rolled oats
♡ 1/2 cup almond milk (or any preferred milk)
♡ One tablespoon molasses
♡ 1/2 teaspoon ground ginger
♡ 1/4 teaspoon ground cinnamon
♡ Pinch of ground cloves
♡ Pinch of salt

Directions:
⚡ Rolling oats, almond milk, molasses, ground ginger, cinnamon, ground cloves, and salt should all be combined in a dish or jar.
⚡ Mix well to blend.
⚡ Refrigerate overnight with a cover on.
⚡ Stir the oats and adjust the sweetness if necessary in the morning.
⚡ As desired, serve warm or cold.

Benefits:
Overnight oats with a gingerbread taste are a great way to boost energy and maintain satiety throughout the morning. They are also a fantastic source of iron, antioxidants, and other critical nutrients that bring back memories of the holiday season.

Berry Crumble Overnight Oats

Ingredients:
♡ 1/2 cup rolled oats
♡ 1/2 cup almond milk (or any preferred milk)
♡ 1/2 cup mixed berries (strawberries, blueberries, raspberries)
♡ One tablespoon of maple syrup or honey
♡ One tablespoon of almond flour or oats
♡ Pinch of cinnamon
♡ Pinch of salt

Directions:
⚡ Rolling oats, almond milk, mixed berries, maple syrup (or honey), almond flour (or oats), cinnamon, and salt should all be combined in a dish or container.
⚡ Mix well to blend.
⚡ Refrigerate overnight with a cover on.
⚡ Stir the oats and adjust the sweetness if necessary in the morning.
⚡ As desired, serve warm or cold.

Benefits:
Berry crumble overnight oats are a tasty blend of acidic and sweet tastes with a crumbly texture. They are also an excellent source of fiber, antioxidants, and other vital nutrients to support general health and encourage fullness throughout the morning.

Lemon Blueberry Overnight Oats

Ingredients:
♡ 1/2 cup rolled oats
♡ 1/2 cup almond milk (or any preferred milk)
♡ Zest and juice of 1/2 lemon
♡ 1/4 cup fresh or frozen blueberries
♡ One tablespoon of maple syrup or honey

♡ Pinch of salt

Directions:
⚡ Rolling oats, almond milk, lemon zest, lemon juice, blueberries, maple syrup (or honey), and salt should all be combined in a bowl or container.
⚡ Mix well to blend.
⚡ Refrigerate overnight with a cover on.
⚡ Stir the oats and adjust the sweetness if necessary in the morning.
⚡ As desired, serve warm or cold.

Benefits:
With the brightness of lemon and the sweetness of blueberries, lemon blueberry overnight oats have a pleasant and tart taste. They also include a fair amount of vitamin C, antioxidants, and other vital nutrients that support immunological health and encourage satiety throughout the morning.

Peaches and Cream Overnight Oats

Ingredients:
♡ 1/2 cup rolled oats
♡ 1/2 cup almond milk (or any preferred milk)
♡ 1/2 ripe peach, diced
♡ One tablespoon Greek yogurt or coconut yogurt
♡ One tablespoon of honey or maple syrup
♡ 1/4 teaspoon vanilla extract
♡ Pinch of cinnamon
♡ Pinch of salt

Directions:
⚡ Rolling oats, almond milk, chopped peach, Greek yogurt (or coconut yogurt), honey (or maple syrup), cinnamon, salt, and vanilla essence should all be combined in a dish or container.
⚡ Mix well to blend.
⚡ Refrigerate overnight with a cover on.

⚡ Stir the oats and adjust the sweetness if necessary in th morning.

⚡ As desired, serve warm or cold.

Benefits:

Peaches and cream overnight oats combine the richness o Greek yogurt with the sweetness of peaches to create a creamy and delicious taste. They also include fiber, probiotics, and other essential nutrients that support gut health and encourage satiety throughout the morning.

Maple Cinnamon Sweet Potato Overnight Oats

Ingredients:

♡ 1/2 cup rolled oats
♡ 1/2 cup almond milk (or any preferred milk)
♡ 1/4 cup mashed sweet potato
♡ One tablespoon of maple syrup
♡ 1/2 teaspoon ground cinnamon
♡ Pinch of nutmeg
♡ Pinch of salt

Directions:

⚡ Combine rolling oats, almond milk, mashed sweet pota maple syrup, nutmeg, ground cinnamon, and salt in a basi or container.

⚡ Mix well to blend.

⚡ Refrigerate overnight with a cover on.

⚡ Stir the oats and adjust the sweetness if necessary in th morning.

⚡ As desired, serve warm or cold.

Benefits:

With the sweetness of maple and the earthiness of sweet potatoes, maple cinnamon sweet potato overnight oats have a warm and soothing taste. They are also a rich source of antioxidants, beta-carotene, and other vital nutrients that support eye health and encourage satiety throughout the morning.

Pomegranate Pistachio Overnight Oats

Ingredients:

- ♡ 1/2 cup rolled oats
- ♡ 1/2 cup almond milk (or any preferred milk)
- ♡ Two tablespoons pomegranate seeds
- ♡ One tablespoon of chopped pistachios
- ♡ One tablespoon of honey or maple syrup
- ♡ 1/4 teaspoon vanilla extract
- ♡ Pinch of cinnamon
- ♡ Pinch of salt

Directions:

⚡ Almond milk, pomegranate seeds, chopped pistachios, honey (or maple syrup), cinnamon, salt, vanilla essence, and rolled oats should all be combined in a dish or container.
⚡ Mix well to blend.
⚡ Refrigerate overnight with a cover on.
⚡ Stir the oats and adjust the sweetness if necessary in the morning.
⚡ As desired, serve warm or cold.

Benefits:

With the sweetness of pomegranate seeds and the nuttiness of pistachios, pomegranate pistachio overnight oats have a crisp and refreshing texture. They are also an excellent source of fiber, antioxidants, and other vital nutrients that support heart health and encourage fullness throughout the morning.

Chocolate Cherry Overnight Oats

Ingredients:

- ♡ 1/2 cup rolled oats
- ♡ 1/2 cup almond milk (or any preferred milk)
- ♡ One tablespoon of cocoa powder
- ♡ One tablespoon of honey or maple syrup
- ♡ 1/4 cup chopped cherries (fresh or frozen)
- ♡ One tablespoon of chopped dark chocolate
- ♡ Pinch of salt

Directions:

⚡ Almond milk, cocoa powder, honey (or maple syrup), chopped cherries, chopped dark chocolate, and salt should all be combined with rolled oats in a dish or jar.
⚡ Mix well to blend.
⚡ Refrigerate overnight with a cover on.
⚡ Stir the oats and adjust the sweetness if necessary in the morning.
⚡ As desired, serve warm or cold.

Benefits:

With the sweetness of cherries and the richness of cocoa, chocolate cherry overnight oats have a rich and luscious taste. They are also an excellent source of fiber, antioxidants and other vital nutrients that support brain function and encourage satiety throughout the morning.

Overnight Oats Parfaits

Enjoy these delicious overnight oats parfaits with their lovely layers of taste and texture. These dishes provide the ideal sweetness ratio to nutrition, making them suitable for every occasion—whether you're searching for a nutritious dessert substitute or an indulgent morning delight.

Berry Blast Parfait:
Alternate layers of Greek yogurt and fresh berries with overnight oats with mixed berries for a colorful and reviving parfait.

Tropical Paradise Parfait:
For a hint of the tropics with every bite, top toasted coconut flakes and chopped pineapple with coconut mango overnight oats.

Chocolate Peanut Butter Parfait:
Layers of chocolate peanut butter overnight oats, sliced bananas, and a dollop of peanut butter will satisfy your sweet taste.

Apple Pie Parfait:
Layers of apple cinnamon overnight oats, diced apples, and a sprinkling of granola for crunch bring you the taste of autumn.

PB&J Parfait:
For a nostalgic take on a beloved recipe, top layers of strawberry chia jam and crushed peanuts on top of peanut butter overnight oats.

Lemon Blueberry Parfait:
Layers of lemon yogurt, fresh blueberries, and overnight oats will provide a zesty sweetness to your morning.

Pumpkin Spice Parfait:
For a fall-inspired dessert, combine layers of pumpkin spice overnight oats, whipped cream, and a dusting of cinnamon to embrace the season's tastes.

Cherry Almond Parfait:
Combine Greek yogurt, chopped almonds, and cherry almond overnight oats to create a delicious, nutty, tangy combo.

Chocolate Raspberry Parfait:
Layers of chocolate raspberry overnight oats, raspberry compote, and dark chocolate shavings will satisfy your chocolate cravings.

Peach Cobbler Parfait:
Layers of peach cobbler overnight oats, vanilla yogurt, and a dusting of cinnamon sugar will transport you to a Southern kitchen.

Maintain the liquid-to-oats ratio:
Aim for a liquid-to-oat ratio of 1:1 or slightly higher for perfectly hydrated and creamy oats.

Experiment with flavors:
Be creative with your toppings and add-ins to keep your overnight oats tasty and exciting. Experiment with various fruits, nuts, seeds, spices, and flavorings to make your oats more appealing.

Sweeten to taste:
You may add honey, maple syrup, or other sweeteners to your overnight oats to make them sweeter to your taste.

Let it soak:
To enable the oats to soften and absorb the flavors, refrigerate your overnight oats for at least four to six hours, or better yet, overnight.

Get creative with toppings:
Sprinkle extra fruit, nuts, seeds, or granola over your overnight oats to enhance taste, texture, and appearance.

Make ahead for busy mornings:
Because they can be made ahead of time and kept in the fridge for up to two or three days, overnight oats are the ideal grab-and-go breakfast choice for hectic mornings.

Customize to dietary preferences:
It's simple to adapt overnight oats to accommodate different dietary requirements, such as vegan, gluten-free, and dairy-free choices.

Have fun and experiment:
Experiment with various flavor combinations and ingredients to make the ideal bowl of overnight oats. Enjoy this adaptable breakfast meal's nourishing and tasty advantages while letting your imagination run wild!

Choose your container wisely:
Because they are easy to travel and store, mason jars are a popular option for overnight oats. However, any container that fits tightly on the lid will work well.

Consider the texture:
You may use less liquid in your recipe if you want thicker oats. On the other hand, you may add a little extra liquid if you wish your oats to be thinner.

Incorporate protein:
If you want your overnight oats to be more balanced and complete, add a protein source like nut butter, Greek yogur or protein powder.

Don't forget the salt:
Though it may not seem like much, a bit of salt can bring o the flavors and counterbalance the sweetness in your overnight oats.

Use flavored liquids:
Try flavoring your yogurt or milk to give your overnight oat more taste depth. You may elevate your oats with flavored yogurt, coconut milk, or vanilla almond milk.

Layer with care:
To guarantee that every mouthful of an overnight oats parf is a balanced combination of tastes and textures, carefully arrange the ingredients equally.

Garnish for visual appeal:
Granola, honey, or fresh fruit slices can add color and visu appeal to your overnight oat parfaits.

Serve chilled:
The best way to eat overnight oats is cold, right out of the fridge. The cold, creamy texture is pleasing and refreshing particularly on warm mornings.

Store properly:
When preparing numerous portions of overnight oats, kee them separate in containers so you can quickly eat them throughout the week. Make sure the lids are securely close to keep the oats fresh.

Get creative:

Don't Feel frees your imagination and novelly combines tastes and ingredients. Because overnight oats are so versatile, feel free to use your creativity and enjoy what you come up with!

Tips for Perfect Overnight Oats

The following advice will help you consistently make delicious overnight oats:

Choose the Right Oats:
Rolling or old-fashioned oats are the finest overnight because they soften nicely when soaked. Steel-cut or fast oats should not be used because they absorb liquid less effectively.

Maintain the Liquid-to-Oats Ratio:
Aim for a liquid-to-oat ratio of 1:1 or slightly higher for perfectly hydrated and creamy oats. Adapt the liquid quantity to your desired consistency.

Use the Right Liquid:
Use yogurt or milk (vegetable or dairy-based) for extra creaminess and taste. You may also use a mixture of milk and yogurt for added richness.

Sweeten to Taste:
Add sweeteners like honey, maple syrup, agave nectar, or brown sugar to make your overnight oats taste even better. Adjust the sweetness to taste by considering the additional ingredients you'll add.

Incorporate Flavor Enhancers:
To give your overnight oats more depth and complexity, try enhancing the taste with vanilla extract, cinnamon, nutmeg, cocoa powder, or almond extract.

Add Nutritional Boosters:
To increase the protein, fiber, and healthy fats in your overnight oats, add chia seeds, flaxseed meal, protein powder, or nut butter.

Mix Well:
Mix the liquid, sweeteners, flavorings, and oats until evenly dispersed to ensure everything is well-mixed. This will guarantee a consistent taste throughout and help avoid clumping.

Experiment with Add-Ins:
Personalize your overnight oats with granola, dried or fresh fruit, nuts, seeds, shredded coconut, chocolate chips, or other add-ins for extra taste, texture, and nutrition.

Store Properly:
Once ready to eat, pour your cooked overnight oats into mason jars or airtight containers and keep them chilled in the fridge. By doing this, you can keep your oats fresh and stop them from absorbing the smells from the refrigerator.

Garnish:
Before serving, add extra garnishes or toppings to preserve their texture and freshness. This may contain spices, nuts, seeds, honey, syrup, and fresh fruit slices.

Experiment and Have Fun:
To discover your go-to overnight oats recipe, don't be scared to be creative and try out various flavor combos and ingredients. Enjoy the process of making delicious and nourishing meals; the options are unlimited!

Keep Healthier

Thanks for being with us

Printed in Great Britain
by Amazon

52204420R00050